Please visit our website, www.enslow.com. For a free color catalog of all our high-quality books, call toll free 1-800-398-2504 or fax 1-877-980-4454.

**Library of Congress Cataloging-in-Publication Data**

Names: Taylor, Charlotte, author.
Title: Celebrating U.S. holidays / Charlotte Taylor.
Description: New York : Enslow Publishing, [2021] | Series: Being a U.S. citizen | Includes index. | Contents: Words to know—Special days—The man with a dream—America's leaders—We remember—A free country—Our nation's workers—Coming to a new land—Honor a veteran—Give thanks.
Identifiers: LCCN 2019050665 | ISBN 9781978517417 (library binding) | ISBN 9781978517394 (paperback) | ISBN 9781978517400 (6 Pack) | ISBN 9781978517424 (ebook)
Subjects: LCSH: Holidays—United States—Juvenile literature.
Classification: LCC GT4803 .T39 2021 | DDC 394.26973—dc23
LC record available at https://lccn.loc.gov/2019050665

Published in 2021 by
**Enslow Publishing**
101 West 23rd Street, Suite #240
New York, NY 10011

Copyright © 2021 Enslow Publishing

Designer: Laura Bowen
Editor: Megan Quick

Photo credits: Cover, pp. 1 (flag), 8 (hat), 18 (flag) Alexander Ryabintsev/Shutterstock.com; cover, pp. 1, 13 (fireworks) mountain beetle/Shutterstock.com; p. 4 ann131313/Shutterstock.com; p. 5 Syda Productions/Shutterstock.com; p. 6 Fibonacci/Wikimedia Commons; p. 7 Bettmann/Contributor/Bettmann/Getty Images; p. 9 Frederic Lewis/Staff/Archive Photos/Getty Images; p. 10 MicroOne/Shutterstock.com; p. 11 MivPiv/iStock/Getty Images Plus/Getty Images; p. 13 (main) Tom Wang/Shutterstock.com; p. 14 Incomible/Shutterstock.com; p. 15 Rawpixel/iStock.com; p. 16 Rowr/Shutterstock.com; p. 17 Davepape/Wikimedia Commons; p. 19 Cheryl Casey/Shutterstock.com; p. 20 Volha Shaukavets/Shutterstock.com; p. 21 fstop123/E+/Getty Images.

Portions of this work were originally authored by Janice Charleston and published as *Our Country's Holidays*. All new material in this edition was authored by Charlotte Taylor.

All rights reserved. No part of this book may be reproduced in any form without permission in writing from the publisher, except by a reviewer.

Printed in the United States of America

Some of the images in this book illustrate individuals who are models. The depictions do not imply actual situations or events.

CPSIA compliance information: Batch #BS20ENS: For further information contact Enslow Publishing, New York, New York, at 1-800-398-2504.

# CONTENTS

Special Days..........................4
The Man with a Dream ..........6
America's Leaders..................8
We Remember.......................10
A Free Country......................12
Our Nation's Workers............14
Coming to a New Land.........16
Honor a Veteran....................18
Give Thanks...........................20
Words to Know.....................22
For More Information............23
Index......................................24

**Boldface** words appear in Words to Know.

## SPECIAL DAYS

Holidays are special times for our country. **National** holidays are a time for all Americans to **celebrate**. Some holidays celebrate special people. Other holidays help us remember important events. We start off every January with a holiday. Happy New Year!

# HOLIDAYS ARE A TIME FOR FAMILIES TO CELEBRATE TOGETHER.

# THE MAN WITH A DREAM

On the third Monday in January, we honor Dr. Martin Luther King Jr. He told people that he had a dream. He wanted people of all colors to be treated the same. Dr. King was an important leader. He fought for a better life for black Americans.

THE LIFE OF MARTIN LUTHER KING JR. TEACHES US TO BE FAIR AND KIND TO EVERYONE.

## AMERICA'S LEADERS

Presidents' Day is on the third Monday in February. At first, this holiday only celebrated George Washington's birthday. Washington was the first American president. Today, it's a day to celebrate all of our presidents. We remember how they have helped our country.

GEORGE WASHINGTON AND ABRAHAM LINCOLN WERE BOTH BORN IN FEBRUARY.

LINCOLN

WASHINGTON

## WE REMEMBER

**Memorial** Day is the last Monday in May. It's a day that we remember the **soldiers** who fought and died for our country. On Memorial Day, people fly American flags and go to parades. Some visit the **graves** of soldiers.

# ON MEMORIAL DAY, WE THINK ABOUT ALL OF OUR BRAVE SOLDIERS.

## A FREE COUNTRY

The Fourth of July is also known as **Independence** Day. We celebrate the day our country was born in 1776. People go to parades and have parties. They play music about America. At night, there are fireworks all around the country.

FIREWORKS LIGHT UP THE NIGHT SKY ON THE FOURTH OF JULY.

# OUR NATION'S WORKERS

Labor Day is the first Monday in September. It's a day to celebrate American workers. Years ago, workers weren't treated well. They got together and **demanded** to be treated better. On Labor Day, we honor Americans' hard work.

# AMERICANS WORK AT MANY DIFFERENT KINDS OF JOBS.

# COMING TO A NEW LAND

Columbus Day is the second Monday in October. Christopher Columbus was an **explorer** from Italy. He tried to sail from Spain to Asia. Instead, Columbus landed in North America in 1492. He thought he had landed in Asia.

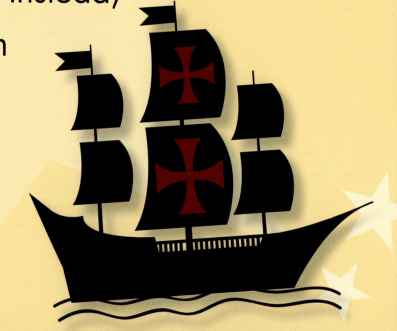

# THERE WERE ALREADY PEOPLE LIVING IN THE AREA WHERE COLUMBUS LANDED.

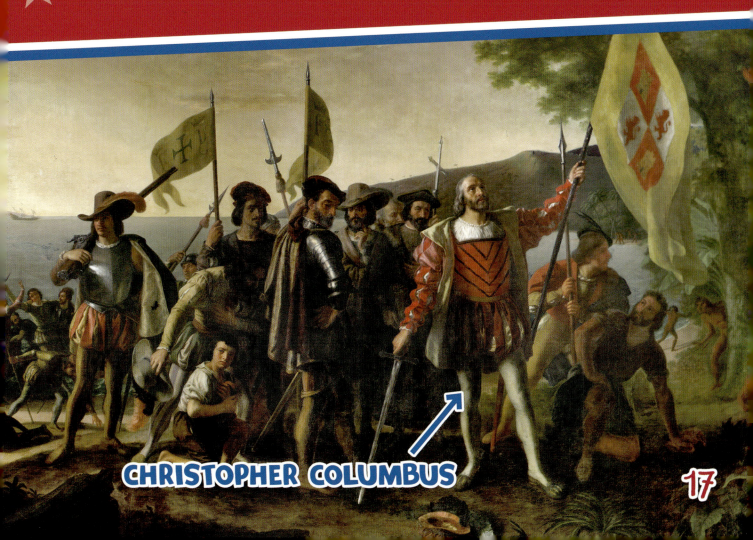

CHRISTOPHER COLUMBUS

## HONOR A VETERAN

On **Veterans** Day, we honor the people who fight for our country. Every year on November 11, we remember the soldiers who have died. We thank the veterans who are still living and those who are serving in the armed forces. They make sure that all Americans are safe and free.

American veterans are the brave men and women who fought for our country.

## GIVE THANKS

Thanksgiving is on the fourth Thursday in November. It's a time to give thanks for the special people and good things in our lives. Many people have a big turkey dinner on Thanksgiving. They give thanks for tasty food!

AT THANKSGIVING, PEOPLE SPEND TIME WITH GOOD FRIENDS AND FAMILY.

# WORDS TO KNOW

**celebrate**  To honor with special activities.
**demand**  To say in a strong way that you have a right to something.
**explorer**  Someone who travels to find new places.
**grave**  The place where a person is buried.
**independence**  Freedom.
**memorial**  Something that is used as a way to remember someone.
**national**  Having to do with the whole country.
**soldier**  A person in the armed forces.
**veteran**  A person who used to serve in the armed forces.

# FOR MORE INFORMATION

## Books

Berne, Emma Carlson. *Fourth of July.* North Mankato, MN: Cantata Learning, 2018.

Seymour, Michaela. *Why Do We Celebrate Martin Luther King Jr. Day?* New York, NY: PowerKids Press, 2018.

## Websites

**All About the Holidays**

nj.pbslearningmedia.org/collection/holidays/
Explore videos about the different holidays throughout the year.

**Holidays**

www.ducksters.com/holidays/kids_calendar.php
Check out a list of holidays and find out why they are celebrated.

**Publisher's note to educators and parents:** Our editors have carefully reviewed these websites to ensure that they are suitable for students. Many websites change frequently, however, and we cannot guarantee that a site's future contents will continue to meet our high standards of quality and educational value. Be advised that students should be closely supervised whenever they access the internet.

# INDEX

Columbus, Christopher, 16

Columbus Day, 16

Fourth of July, 12

Independence Day, 12

King, Martin Luther, Jr., 6

Labor Day, 14

Memorial Day, 10

national holidays, 4

presidents, 8

Presidents' Day, 8

soldiers, 10, 18

Thanksgiving, 20

veterans, 18

Veterans Day, 18

Washington, George, 8

workers, 14